The Adventures of Biff and Griff

David McCarthy

The Adventures of Biff and Griff

David McCarthy

Copyright © 2024 David McCarthy. All Rights Reserved.

Published by David McCarthy

ISBN 979-8-218-45895-9

New Paws, New Adventures

The adventures began when two sisters stepped out of their car and were greeted by the sight of a quaint, cozy house with a cheerful red door.

The overcast sky seemed to add a touch of magic to the air, and a few raindrops gently pattered against the ground.

Excitement tingled in the air as the sisters made their way to the front door, ready to meet their new furry family members.

"Griff! Biff!" called out one of the sisters with a delighted grin, and instantly, two bundles of fur turned the corner and came bounding toward them. Biff, with his mischievous eyes and a patch over the right, wagged his tail furiously. Griff, less enthused, had to be carried outside.

Once outside, the puppies were now both brimming with excitement. Their tails wagging like metronomes set to the rhythm of pure joy.

With a flurry of licks and wagging tails, Biff and Griff were gently lifted into the car. They snuggled up close to each other, finding comfort in their brotherly bond.

The car ride was an adventure itself. The brothers pressed their noses against the window, taking in the world passing by. They saw cars zipping along the road, houses with colorful gardens, and even a big, friendly dog with floppy ears sticking out of a car window, wagging its tail enthusiastically.

Finally, the car pulled up in front of Biff's new home. As soon as the car door opened, the two pups tumbled out onto the lush green grass. With barks of joy, they chased each other around the yard, their paws dancing on the soft earth. They rolled, wrestled, and played, their laughter echoing around the yard.

Toys of all shapes and sizes awaited them—squeaky bones, fluffy balls, and a stuffed bear that was bigger than they were. They tugged and tossed the toys around, sharing playful growls and excited barks.

Soon, more members of the family emerged from the house. Biff and Griff's tails wagged even faster as they met their new human family members. Laughter filled the air as they were showered with cuddles and affection.

After hours of playful adventures, it was time for Griff to take another ride to his new house. With a final round of tail wags, the brothers bid each other goodnight, eager to start their new lives with their loving families.

And as the sun set on the first day with their families, Biff and Griff drifted off to sleep, dreaming of the exciting adventures that awaited them in their new homes.

Today was a Great Day!

Paw-some Park Adventure

As the car rolled smoothly along the road, Griff's excitement bubbled over. He knew it was Saturday—the special day when he got to spend time with his brother, Biff.

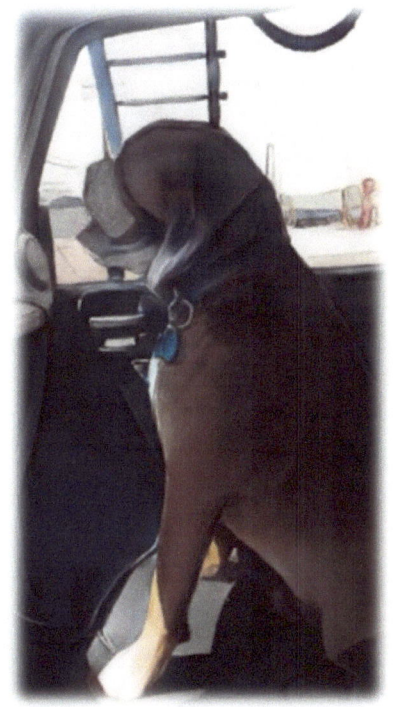

The sun shone brightly, casting a warm glow over the neighborhood, and Griff couldn't wait for the day's adventure.

As they turned into the dog park parking lot, Griff's tail wagged furiously. His nose twitched with anticipation, catching a familiar scent that made his heart leap with joy.

There, among the fluttering leaves and playful breeze, stood Biff! Griff yipped happily and rushed towards his brother, their tails wagging in unison.

Bounding towards the entrance, the two brothers could barely contain their excitement. They practically dragged their owners along the path, their paws barely touching the ground.

The moment they dashed through the gates into the dog park, it was like they had entered a world of endless play.

Dogs of all shapes, sizes, and colors greeted them. Griff and Biff wasted no time, joining the joyful chaos of canine companions.

They raced around, chasing and being chased, their excited energy filling the park.

But then, amidst the excitement, Biff's keen eyes spotted something intriguing. At the bottom of the hill lay a muddy puddle, its glistening surface calling out to them. With a mischievous glance at Griff, Biff bolted toward the mud puddle, his brother right on his tail.

They leaped into the mud with wild abandon, rolling and splashing, their fur quickly turning shades of brown. Their owners laughed, watching the brothers reveling in their messy adventure.

As their time at the park drew to a close, their owners guided them towards a nearby creek. With a dip into the cool, flowing water, Griff and Biff rinsed off some of the mud, shaking off droplets in a joyful dance.

Once back home, bath time awaited them. Biff and Griff splashed around in the sudsy water, their owners giggling at their playful antics. Scrubbed clean and smelling fresh, the tired but content pups nestled into their cozy beds, eyelids growing heavy with the day's excitement.

Exhausted from the day's playful escapades, Biff and Griff snuggled close, their hearts full of love for each other, and drifted off into a dream-filled slumber, eagerly awaiting their next adventure together.

Today was a Great Day!

Diving In: Adventure of learning to Swim

Under the blazing summer sun, the air shimmered with warmth as the sounds of laughter and splashing filled the backyard. Biff and Griff lounged on the grass beside the shimmering pool, panting in the heat. Their tongues lolled out happily, but soon, the heat became too much for them.

Watching the dogs, their owners exchanged knowing glances. "I think it's time," one of them said with a smile. With a gentle nudge, they coaxed Biff towards the pool's edge. With a gleeful bark, Biff jumped right in, the cool water enveloping him in a refreshing embrace. He paddled happily, feeling the relief wash over him.

On the other hand, Griff hesitated at the water's edge, uncertain of what awaited him. He had never been in water this deep before. He glanced at Biff, who was enjoying himself, but Griff's nerves held him back.

Sensing Griff's uncertainty, his human dad knelt down and gently lifted him into the water, supporting him as he found his footing. The moment Griff's paws touched the water's surface, instinct kicked in. His legs started paddling, almost as if they knew what to do without his conscious thought.

Griff was astonished as he glided through the water effortlessly. He kicked and splashed, discovering the thrill of swimming for the first time. Yet, despite the exhilaration, a sense of unease lingered within him. He swam towards the steps, seeking solace in the familiarity of solid ground.

Meanwhile, Biff, having explored the pool's depths, made his way to the steps, his eyes shining with the joy of the new experience. He joined Griff on the warm concrete, basking in the sun's rays and enjoying the gentle breeze that rustled the leaves nearby.

As the day unfolded, the dogs lounged contentedly, their wet fur drying in the sun. The clear blue sky stretched above them as they relished the company of their human family, the memory of their swimming adventure leaving them with tails wagging happily.

Today was a Great Day!

The Adventure of A Buzzworthy Discovery

In the lush backyard of CC and Pap's house, the air buzzed with excitement as Biff and Griff romped and played, their tails wagging in unison. The vibrant green grass provided the perfect playground for the two brothers, their playful antics a joy to watch for everyone who gathered for a family lunch.

Amidst the laughter and conversation, the dogs suddenly froze, their ears perked and noses twitching in alertness. Something in the air had caught their attention. With a sense of curiosity, they began to sniff around, their inquisitive nature taking over.

Biff's keen nose picked up a faint scent, and he darted towards a small hole in the ground. His snout ventured into the mysterious opening, but within seconds, he recoiled in surprise, sprinting away in a flash, his tail tucked between his legs.

Perplexed by Biff's sudden dash, Griff approached the hole, trying to comprehend what had startled his brother. Intrigued, he cautiously poked his nose into the opening. Suddenly, a chorus of buzzing filled the air, growing louder and more intense. Before Griff could make sense of the commotion, a sharp pinch stung his nose, causing him to leap back, startled, and bolt away in alarm.

Observing the dogs' reactions, the humans exchanged puzzled glances. Curiosity piqued, they ventured closer to the hole. As they neared, they spotted bees hovering near the ground, their wings fluttering rapidly. "The dogs found a bees' nest!" one of the humans exclaimed, now understanding.

Sensing the potential danger, the humans knew they had to act swiftly to keep the dogs safe. "Who wants a treat?" one called out, trying to distract Biff and Griff from their newfound discovery.

At the sound of those magical words, the dogs' ears perked up, their attention diverted from the intriguing hole. With tails wagging in excitement, Biff and Griff eagerly followed the humans, their noses still tingling from the unexpected encounter.

Although tempted to explore further, the promise of a tasty treat lured Biff and Griff away from the bees' nest. Relieved, their human parents guided them away, ensuring their safety as they retreated from the potential hazard.

As the dogs happily savored their treats, the humans chuckled at the day's unexpected adventure. Biff and Griff, although momentarily intrigued by the bees, were content with their treats and the loving company of their family, leaving the buzzing mystery behind them.

Today was a Great Day!

Frosty Fun: A Snow Day Adventure

As the night fell, Griff peered out the window alongside his human sibling, wondering if Biff was doing the same thing at his house. The sky was aglow with the soft light of the moon, casting a serene aura over the world below. They watched in wonder as large, fluffy snowflakes danced gracefully from the heavens, swirling and twirling in the chilly night air.

Their parents had mentioned a storm on its way, promising a blanket of snow by morning. The anticipation hung thick in the air as the family retired for the night, dreams filled with visions of snow-covered landscapes.

The next morning, a magical sight awaited them. With sleepy eyes and wide smiles, everyone hurried to the window. The world outside was transformed, bathed in a pristine layer of shimmering snow that glistened in the morning sunlight.

Breakfast was a flurry of excitement, and hurried munching, as the children eagerly anticipated their snowy adventure. Bundling up felt like an eternity—the layers of coats, scarves, and mittens seemed to take forever to arrange just right.

Finally, all bundled up, Griff and the children gathered by the garage door, the anticipation palpable. With a swift lift, the door rolled up, and Griff wasted no time bolting into the winter wonderland, followed closely by the excited children.

A short while later, a familiar vehicle pulled into the driveway. "It was Biff and his family," Griff thought. The doors opened and everyone burst out in a hurry. Laughter filled the crisp air as they all plunged into the snowy playground. Together, they crafted a jolly snowman, giggling as they adorned it with a carrot nose, a hat, and scarf.

Sleds were brought out, and gleeful shrieks echoed through the air as they raced down the snow-covered slope. Biff and Griff chased after snowballs, the soft mounds disappearing into the powdery snow as they landed, leaving the dogs playfully searching for their lost targets.

After a while, their cheeks rosy and noses cold, they headed inside, breathless from their snow-filled escapades. The children shed their snowy attire while Biff and Griff patiently awaited their turn for a thorough brushing to remove the snow that had clung to their furry coats.

The children savored steaming cups of hot chocolate, their eyes sparkling with delight, while the dogs rested contentedly, their fur still damp and a hint of snow lingering in their paws. As they curled up to rest, memories of their snowy adventures danced in their dreams, cherishing the joy of their day in the winter wonderland.

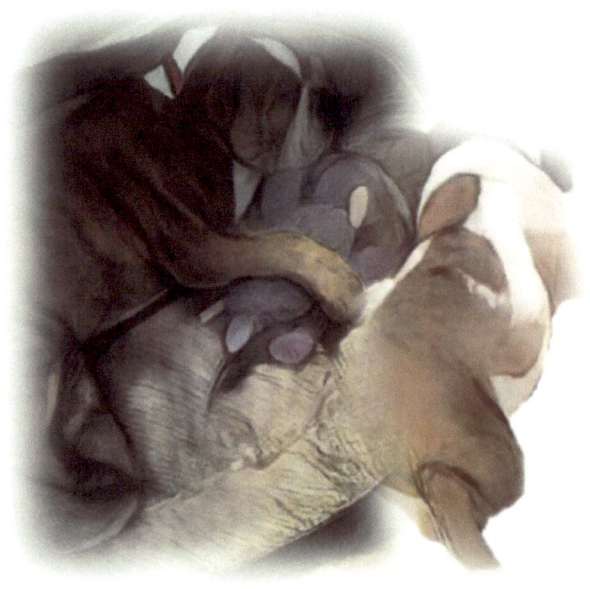

Today was a Great Day!

Sun, Sand, and Sea: A Magical Beach Adventure

As the golden hues of dawn painted the sky, Biff and Griff stirred from their slumber, eager for the adventure that awaited them. The fresh scent of the ocean air drifted through the crack in the door, teasing their sensitive noses and making them want to go outside.

Their tails wagged in anticipation as their parents announced they were going for a walk on the beach. Biff and Griff practically danced with excitement, their paws tapping eagerly on the floor.

Bounding along the walkway towards the beach, the dogs strained at their leashes, their enthusiasm barely contained. As they stepped onto the sandy shore, their paws sunk into the cool, damp sand, sending a thrill through their bodies.

The beach lay quiet in the early morning, the rhythmic crash of waves providing a soothing soundtrack. Biff and Griff gazed around, eager to explore the vast stretch of sand and sea. However, their parents asked them to sit, and confusion flickered in the dogs' eyes. "Why are we sitting?" they wondered.

With a mischievous twinkle in their eyes, their parents unclipped the leashes and exclaimed, "Go ahead!" With a burst of joy, Biff and Griff dashed off, their paws kicking up sand behind them.

They sniffed at crab holes and washed-up seaweed before sprinting towards the water's edge. As they approached, a wave surged forward, and the dogs hesitated, retreating from the advancing water. They watched in awe as the foamy water receded, leaving behind shells and sea treasures.

With a newfound cautiousness, they dipped their paws into the shallows, feeling the cool embrace of the ocean. They romped and frolicked at the water's edge, chasing each other as waves rolled in and out.

After an exhilarating play in the surf, they reluctantly bid farewell to the beach and headed back to their beach house.

Lounging by the pool, they sought refuge from the sun's heat. The day passed in lazy contentment, the dogs basking in the shade and occasionally venturing into the refreshing water to cool their sun-warmed fur.

As the day waned and the sun dipped towards the horizon, Biff and Griff retreated to the cool floor inside. Dreams filled with the sights, sounds, and smells of their adventurous day at the beach filled their minds leaving them eager for more seaside escapades in the days to come.

Today was a Great Day!

www.ingramcontent.com/pod-product-compliance
Lightning Source LLC
Chambersburg PA
CBHW040949050426
42337CB00048B/59